Mou
Rushmore

An American Symbol

Alison and Stephen Eldridge

Enslow Elementary
an imprint of

Enslow Publishers, Inc.
40 Industrial Road
Box 398
Berkeley Heights, NJ 07922
USA

http://www.enslow.com

Enslow Elementary, an imprint of Enslow Publishers, Inc.
Enslow Elementary® is a registered trademark of Enslow Publishers, Inc.

Library of Congress Cataloging-in-Publication Data
Eldridge, Alison.
  Mount Rushmore : an American symbol / by Alison and Stephen Eldridge.
    p. cm. — (All about American symbols)
  Includes bibliographical references and index.
  Summary: "Introduces pre-readers to simple concepts about Mt. Rushmore using short sentences and
repetition of words"—Provided by publisher.
  ISBN 978-0-7660-4060-1
  1. Mount Rushmore National Memorial (S.D.)—Juvenile literature. I. Eldridge, Stephen. II. Title.
  F657.R8E43 2012
  978.3'93—dc23
                              2011032900
Future editions:
Paperback ISBN 978-1-4644-0049-0
ePUB ISBN 978-1-4645-0956-8
PDF ISBN 978-1-4645-0956-5

Printed in China
012012 Leo Paper Group, Heshan City, Guangdong, China
10 9 8 7 6 5 4 3 2 1

Note to Parents and Teachers

Help pre-readers get a jump start on reading. These lively stories introduce simple concepts with
repetition of words and short simple sentences. Photos and illustrations fill the pages with color and
effectively enhance the text. Free Educator Guides are available for this series at www.enslow.com.
Search for the *All About American Symbols* series name.

Contents

Words to Know

 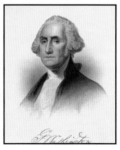 

mountain   president   symbol

I see Mount Rushmore.

Mount Rushmore is a mountain.

Mount Rushmore is a symbol of America.

What does it make you think of?

Mount Rushmore makes you think of great Americans.

George
Washington

Thomas
Jefferson

It has the faces of four presidents.

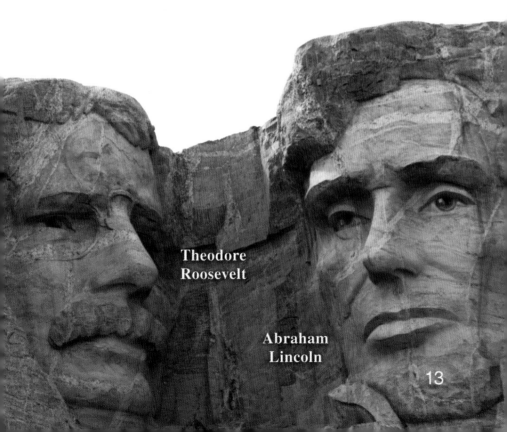

Theodore
Roosevelt

Abraham
Lincoln

Workmen on face of
Geo Washington
mt. Rushmore

RISE STU
RAPID C
S DA

A man cut the faces
in the stone.

It took 14 years to make it!

Where do I see Mount Rushmore?

I see Mount Rushmore in South Dakota.

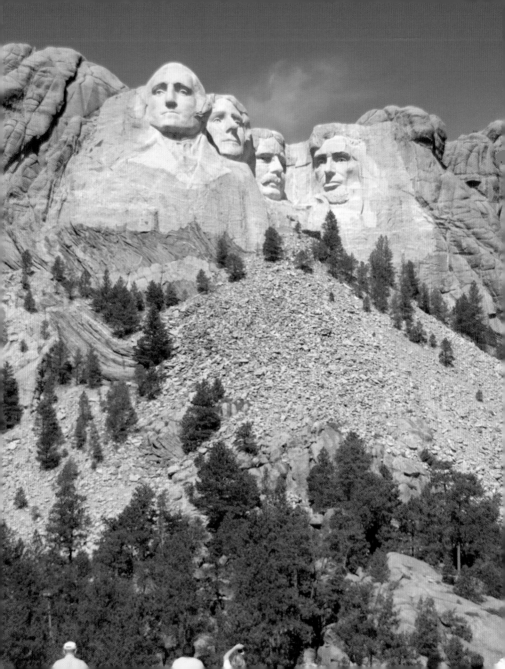

I see Mount
Rushmore.

I think of America!

Read More

Bodden, Valerie. *Mount Rushmore.* Mankato, Minn.: Creative Education, 2007.

Jango-Cohen, Judith. *Mount Rushmore.* Minneapolis, Minn.: Lerner Publications Company, 2004.

Rau, Dana Meachen. *Mount Rushmore.* Minneapolis, Minn.: Compass Point Books, 2002.

Web Sites

Ben's Guide to U.S. Government for Kids. *Statues and Memorials: Mount Rushmore.* <http://bensguide.gpo.gov/3-5/symbols/mountrushmore.html>

U.S. National Park Service. *Mount Rushmore—For Kids.* <http://www.nps.gov/moru/forkids/index.htm>

Index

Guided Reading Level: **B**
Guided Reading Leveling System is based on the guidelines recommended by Fountas and Pinnell.

Word Count: 73